PAST PRESENT

Piers Plowless

&

Sir Orfeo

Maureen Duffy

The Pottery Press

First published in London in 2017 by
The Pottery Press
Potters' Yard
116 Lady Margaret Road
London N19 5EX

www.pottersyard.co.uk

New edition 2019

ISBN: 978-0-9930171-1-7

A CIP record for this book
is available from the British Library

Designed in Perpetua by The Pottery Press
Printed in England by Imprint Digital

Past Present: Piers Plowless & Sir Orfeo

Foreword

The New Vision of Piers Plowless is Maureen Duffy's contemporary riff on the medieval poem, The Vision of Piers Plowman, which combines social protest and satire with allegory about the pilgrimage of the soul, and a vision of England transformed.

Duffy is a worthy inheritor of this epic English form, in the line of poetic forebears she invokes from Chaucer and Shakespeare to Woolf, Eliot and, especially, Blake. Blake's vision of London as the new Jerusalem, a place of visions and nightmares, is ever-present in Duffy's London trilogy of novels and her poetry, and in this long poem it inspires her to a magnificent rant, addressed to fellow-author Will Langland who wrote his protest song for everyman Piers and 'the fair field of folk' so many centuries ago.

Her protest against a so-called austerity which causes suffering to the poorest in society while sparing the richest, and tries to silence the arts and deplete learning and libraries, has never been more relevant. But crucially, like her medieval model, there's robust humour here too – and a breath of hope; a call to arms.

Sir Orfeo, its companion here, is Maureen Duffy's translation of another medieval English poem, which migrates the Orpheus myth to the England of a folktale, and gives it a happy ending. The classical Underworld becomes Elfland under a green hill, the Arcadian landscape an English orchard.

Duffy's own introduction to the poem's history places it within a singer-songwriter or troubador context, and her skilful translation catches the energy and rhythm of the original, its narrative immediacy and sturdy language, so that the reader experiences it as a bardic re-telling in that truly folk idiom.

In **Past Present** the coupling of these two poems makes a weird and powerful statement about England on the edge; a land with an imagined mythic past, a millennial present and perhaps apocalyptic future.

The lettered title pages and the images for Sir Orfeo are by lettering artist Liz Mathews, who has worked with Maureen Duffy's poetry before, notably in Paper Wings (also published by The Pottery Press in 2014). Atmospheric colour-studies rather than illustrations, they accompany the text, dreamlike and evocative.

Frances Bingham, London 2017

The New Vision of Piers Plowless

Ho Piers, Peterkin, you hover on the edge
of our consciousness as I follow your footsteps
living in London and on London as you did
or rather your maker that Long Will with Kit
his wife on Cornhill, exercising his trade
not willing to dig or delve, as poets still
demand the right to write. But I can't say
services for bread, only offer my words
propped up by day jobs, like Chaucer, ambassador
for whichever king, wheedling his way to kickstart
English Lit, while you my dear gave what?
Blessings for a groat, counsel, shrivings, masses?
Never mind Will (if your bones can) though he's
on the syllabus, you're there too, no courtier, just
versing the way of the world and now we need you
again. Those ills, greed and lust, ride high once more
roughshod, and where's your Piers to stay them?
Will he come if I invoke him, dropping
his holy shift, attuned to our more sumptuous

secular times? I can show him a world so like
his own he'll say, 'Has nothing changed? Is all
I said before been so much smoke, no fire in
the belly to burn away the dross but inky
parchment bonds and blots?' Should I die
proclaiming it? And England's green and pleasant
land with playing fields housed over, 'the whole boiling
bricked in' as one of your unwilling successors
said, and those poor you saw not singing anymore
at the pub but out for a furtive shot on the corner
that's cheaper. Did you think it would all change
as we did post our war, with your words? Remember
as the man said, 'Poetry, art, makes nothing happen.'
Yet we try, banging our heads against our keyboards
now, crying, 'We're all still here in the field
full of folk and you, wherever you are, call us
to till your half-acre, meaning bend our backs
to whatever seems a straight furrow.'
'What can you do?' Reason asked you and asks us still.
And I would answer: 'I can write,' as you said
you could pray, not knowing your words would be
echoing still a millennium on. So to that fair field
of folk. Survey it. Has much changed? There's binge
drinking as yours sat and sang, and lager for ale.

Lady Meed

And Lady Meed? Oh she still rides out clad in bankers'
bonuses, except we're the asses to carry their load.

And the poor who are with us always? We've hardened
our hearts towards them, bidding them take up
your challenge to dig and delve with labour according
to their talents, with the halt, the lame and the blind.
Would you ask us Peterkin to whip them into shape?
No, you would have had compassion as some still do
even if they don't share that Christ who taught you
to care. But Lady Meed, now there's an immortal.
You'll know her though she's dressed in the paper
rags that hide her gold-hardened heart, cold as milled
steel that can't be pierced by cries of poverty and need.
No contriteness cloaks her for plunging us into the dark
with the poorest to bear her burden on bent backs
while she tramples them underfoot. I see them stream
as in Blake's darkest dream over London Bridge:
women with baby at breast and toddler at hand
bag ladies, doorway dossers, my window cleaner
'let go', now joined by every walk and age
and colour, scholars in flapping gowns, pin-striped
bureaucrats, who never thought the axe could fall
on them, cry out in pain, while those more used
to Lady Fortune's frown just grit their teeth.
Past gherkin and towering glass and steel they stream
holding their hands up against the bitter sky
while statesmen sum and subtract and politicians
probe lives they know nothing of, safe in their
seats padded with Daddy's money or the firm
to bail them out. Sequestered since childhood

in cushioned enclaves they come in the train
of Lady Meed, straddling their high horses
to admonish us: 'Carve up nothing into smaller bites
to fill the belly.' And no one comes to harrow this
hell and lead us into the light, no one to heal
our sick and raise our dead, touch lepers of mind
or body, suffer the children with free milk and meals.
Get us to share our broken bread and fish. Instead
we're set against each other, sister on sister
whose skin's a different colour but I was taught
'The world's my country.' You didn't have this
problem, Piers, of a world on the move. How would
you have dealt if the Ottoman came to your door?

The Muses

Now see as a nightmare by Fuseli out of Blake
or Gilray and Hogarth rolled up in one: Britannia
devouring her children: clerks in black suits, Slasher
Trimmer and Cut, steel points poised above notepads
going their rounds. A group of girls, nine, danced
in a stately ring. 'Now subsidy sluts go off, stack
shelves, pick fruit. You there Terpsichore, put on
these smart red shoes embroidered with pain
and grief. What's that? Too small! Cut off your toes.
They'll dance you til you drop. Euterpe, now
what's all that noise? We'll dock your strings
and have some quiet here so we can hear the chink
of bankers' bonuses. You want for cash? Ask them.

See if they'll fund your squawkings. And you
Melpomene, what do you do to keep yourself
but pander to the worst with tales of blood and lust.
Erato, Polyhymnia and Calliope: what three
to do one job, scribble a few lines for idle girls?
We don't need history, Clio. We live in modern
times. Star gazing Urania? Where's the call for that?
What ends does it serve now? What profits return?'
So they went on til only Thalia was left
working the stand-up circuit in half empty pubs
where Sorrow drowns in lager swills until she
staggers out, falls in the gutter and there's
no A&E to take her in.

Then on again in glee went Slasher, Trimmer, Cut
chanting 'We are the Treasury Boys; we come
to trim your fat,' past shuttered libraries, dark stages,
silent concert halls and emptied galleries
where once the nation's pictures hung, flogged off
to pay the debt. So up and down they run
exhorting us to labour at broken weaving looms
in shuttered mines where the grass grows over
abandoned slagheaps, shipyards where work's dry
docked, steel mills whose fires went out, all trades
exported off to cheaper hands and Gaunt's harsh
prophecies come home to roost bound up in mergers
contracts of unemployment, outsourcings
and Hypocrite weeps: 'So sorry to let you go.'

Piers Plowless

The Muses turned to Piers who shook his head.
'There's nothing I can do. I'm Piers Jobseeker now.
My land's sold off for gated second homes since
what we eat comes mainly from abroad. Farming's
an industry for agribis not yeomen smallholders
like me. Even the poor cows can't lactate fast
enough to earn their keep.' 'Surely,' they cried
'you've fields of strawberries or apples we could
gather, just as the axemen said.' 'The pickers
come each year as once we gathered hops.
They're used to it. They sleep in dormitories
or caravans for a pittance and their board.
No mortgages to pay or kids to school. Then
it's back home where pounds notch up more
than their native euros. You couldn't keep it up
hour after hour filling a thousand punnets.
Your backs would crack, your hands aren't swift
and tough but fashioned to other work where
your skills can shine to highlight truth and beauty
to other lives.' Melpomene struck her breast.
'Are we to be again then only rich men's
toys, just players for patrons, dubbed elitist
through no choice of our own. I will resist!'
But sweetvoiced Euterpe gave tongue. 'What choice
have we; even caged birds sing?' With drooping
heads they drift away, and when I look again
even Peterkin is gone, sucked into the throng

on London Bridge with now another 150,000 strong
or weak and more each day, far as the eye can see
their shuffling feet, like Wasteland dead undone
can scarcely rock the bridge so slow they move
each pressed against her neighbour. But then comes

Flatterer

Flatterer the mouthpiece, to gull the people
with fear and oily phrases, calling them salt
of the earth who will rescue the land as their fathers
did before them, tightening their belts til all
acquiesce in their chains of poverty, hunger
conning them with promises of a common pain
freemen become slaves to bonds and bankruptcy
hedge-funded about with a maze not of their making.

Jerusalem Fallen

And where is our Piers who can set all to rights?
Where should we search for him? Among the brash
young hopefuls with their management speak, or
look up to the moneymen and abandon the poor?
Who'll build us Jerusalem? But nobody answers
out of the crowd of fearful self-seekers. Until
suddenly, weeping, Piers pushes forward, snaps
his shining arrows of desire in two, unstrings
his golden bow, hurling his spear at the sun
as darkness descends. And I awake in Fulham
and take up my pen to follow your tracks.

Sir Orfeo

Introduction: Sir Orfeo

Sir Orfeo belongs to that long tradition in English of fairy literature which stretches from Old English elf shot and the marsh monsters Grendel and his mother, down through the centuries via Spenser's Fairy Queen and Keats' La Belle Dame Sans Merci to the science fictions of Star Wars and Doctor Who.

The earliest extant manuscript (Auchinleck MS Edinburgh National Library of Scotland, Advocates 19) appears to have been written by some half a dozen scribes in around 1330-40, along with 43 other lays, romances, homilies and other pieces, including a version of Guy of Warwick, in a dialect of South Midlands, London. It retells the Greek myth of Orpheus and Eurydice but, like Gluck's Orpheo, it has a happy ending. In form it derives in conscious imitation from the poetic tradition of the lai, popularised by Breton singer-songwriters and translated post-Conquest into Britain, the most famous proponent of which is Marie de France, whose La Freyne also appears in the Auchinleck MS and with which Sir Orfeo shares its first 38 lines, making obeisance to Breton lays and placing itself firmly in that tradition, perhaps in the hope of a wider audience at this time when English was still in competition with French and Latin as an acceptable literary language.

Its roots are, however, deep in the English faery/folk tradition which continued, some would say in debased form, in the later ballads like Tam Lin and True Thomas. The English version of the myth transfers the locus of the story firmly to England. Sir Orfeo isn't the son of Apollo but King of Winchester, and the finest harper in the world, still with the power to enchant men and beasts with his music. Eurydice, his queen Herodis, is stolen by the Fairy King into the parallel world of Fairyland which exists in another dimension into which mortals can stray by a simple but foolish act such as falling asleep, as Herodis does, at a May noontide under an apple tree. Instead of the gloomy world of Eurydice's Hades however, she finds herself in a richly decorated palace where the undead can follow their earthly sports of hawking, hunting and even dancing. We might now indeed call this a virtual world.

In praise of the profession of minstrel, and written to be performed by one, the poem has the effect of a kind of Chinese box or Russian doll, turning in upon itself so that the happy ending seems right, even though Orfeo achieves it by a trick rather than the simple power of song. Returning to his kingdom in disguise he plays another trick, on the steward he has left in charge to test his loyalty. From being a tragic tale of lost love, English has transformed the legend into a parable of virtue and cunning rewarded.

Maureen Duffy, London

We often read and find them writ,

as learned men know so well,

tales that tell of faery things

in the lays that harpers sing.

Some are of war and some of sorrow,

some are of joy and laughter too,

and some of treachery and guile,

of old adventures long ago,

and some of fun and ribaldry

but many you'll find tell of the faery.

Yet most of them, as all agree,

tell tales of love as we can see.

In Brittany these lays were made,

found there first, and soon brought forth,

tales of adventures in olden days

of these the Bretons made their lays.

When kings heard from anywhere

of marvellous happenings that were there

they took a harp and let music play

and out of it they made a lay,
and gave it a name as I can say.
Now of these adventures that did befall
I can tell you some, though not all.
But listen Sirs, all that are true
and I shall tell you of Sir Orfeo.
Orfeo most of anything
loved the pleasure of harping.
Every good harper was certain sure
to have from him great honour.
He taught himself to play the harp
and thereto bent his wits so sharp.
He learned until nowhere was there
a better harper anywhere.
No man alive in all the world,
who, once he sat down before the king,
and could hear his sweet playing
but would think that he was
in one of the halls of paradise
such melody in his harping is.
Orfeo himself was a king
in England, a high lording
a brave man, and stalwart too,
generous and courteous also.
His father was descended from King Pluto
and his mother also from Queen Juno
that were once held to be both gods
for the deeds that they did that were told of them.

This king lived in the land of Thrace
in a splendid battlemented palace.
But Winchester it was called
without a doubt as I've been told.
The king had a precious queen,
Lady Herodis was her name,
the fairest lady she was indeed
that was ever seen alive.
So full of love and nobility
that no one could describe her beauty.
It happened in the beginning of May
when hot and lovely is the day
and away have fled old winter's showers
and every field is full of flowers,
and blossom breaks on every bough
and over all bright colours glow,
this same queen, Dame Herodis,
taking with her two highborn maids
went out in the mid morning fair
to play beside an orchard there,
to see the flowers spread and spring,
and to hear the small birds sing.
And there they sat them down all three
under a fine grafted apple tree.
And very soon this lovely queen
fell asleep upon the green.
Her maidens dared not waken her
but let her lie and take her rest.

It happened in the beginning of May

She scratched her face til it bled wet

And so she slept til after noon
and all the morning time was gone.
But as soon as she began to wake
she cried aloud, and a shrill sound began to make.
She twisted her hands and even her feet.
She scratched her face til it bled wet.
Her rich gown she tore in bits,
she was quite driven out of her wits.
The two maidens at her side
no longer with her dared abide,
but ran to the palace straight away
and told both knight and squire
their queen had run quite mad that day,
and begged them to go and her restrain.
Knights and ladies together ran,
damsels sixty and more
came to the orchard to the queen,
and in their arms their queen they bore
and carried her home to bed at last,
and held her there so firm and fast.
But ever she let out the same cry
and struggled hard to be up and away.
When Orfeo heard all that sad news
never had he heard anything worse.
He came to her with knights then,
to the chamber before the queen,
and saw and said in great distress:
"Oh my dear life what can be wrong

that you who've always been so calm
now cry out in shrill alarm?
Your body once so fair and white
is now all torn with your nails' spite.
Alas your cheeks that were so red
are now so wan as you were dead.
And your little fingers also
are all pale and bloody too.
And your two bright eyes both
glare as a man may in his wrath.
Ah lady I beg you mercy.
Leave off this doleful cry
and tell me what befell you, and how,
and what can be done to help you now."
Then the queen she lay still at last
and began to let the tears run fast.
"Alas my Lord, Sir Orfeo,
since we were first together so,
never were we angry with each other,
but always I loved you faithfully,
as my life. So you did me.
But now we may not be together, we two.
Do your best with it for I must go."
"Alas," he cried, "so desolate as I am.
Where will you go, and to whom?
Wherever you go I will go with thee,
and wherever I go you shall be with me."
"No, no Sir that cannot be.

I'll tell you now how it came to be.
As I lay down this midday
and slept under our orchard's spray,
there came to me two knights
both well armed and all to rights,
and bade me come in great haste
and with the Lord their King hold speech.
But I answered them very bold
that I dare not, nor I would.
They rode back as fast as they could.
Then comes their King to me in haste
with one hundred knights at least,
and a hundred maidens with him too,
all on steeds as white as snow,
their garments were as milk all white.
Never before did I see such a sight,
of lovely beings so fair and bright.
The King bore a crown upon his head
which wasn't of silver nor gold so red,
but was made of some precious stone
that shone as brightly as the sun.
As soon as he came up to me
whether I would or not my hand he seized
and made me with him ride
on a palfrey by his side
and brought me then to his palace,
well set up with every grace.
He showed me castles and tall towers,

rivers, forests, woods with flowers,
and every one of his rich estates.
Then back he brought me home again
to our very own orchard gates.
And right then he said to me:
'See lady that tomorrow you be
right here under this apple tree,
and with us you shall go
and live with us for evermore.
And if you resist with hindrance or let
wherever you are you will be fetched,
and all your limbs shall be tore apart
so that nothing then can help your hurt,
and though you may be mangled thus,
you'll still be carried away with us!' "
When King Orfeo heard all this,
"Oh woe," he said, "alas, alas.
I would rather lose my life
than so to lose the queen, my wife."
He asked advice of every man
but help from any was there none.
Next day when morning time had come,
and Orfeo took up his weapons
with well ten hundred knights along
armed to the teeth, all brave and strong,
then with the queen they took their way
to the apple tree and there did stay
making a shield wall on every side,

and vowed that there they would abide
and die there every one
before the queen should go there from,
and yet from there among them all
the queen was snatched within the wall,
by faery magic stolen away,
where she has gone no man can say.
Then was there crying, weeping and woe.
Into his chamber went Orfeo.
Often he fainted on the stone floor.
Lamenting and in weeping so sore
his life was nearly spent with grief,
nor could he find there any relief.
He called together his barons,
earls and lords of great renown
and when they were assembled there
"Sirs," he said, "before you here
I empower my steward faithfully
to rule my kingdom after me.
In my stead he shall stand
now to govern all my land,
for now my queen is lost to me,
I shall nevermore woman see.
Into the wilderness I shall go
there to live forevermore,
in the ancient forests with the wild beasts,
and when you know I am deceased,
call Parliament to sit and choose

a new king for all of my affairs;
so do your best with all my cares."
Then there was weeping in the hall
and a great cry rose up from them all.
Young nor old could speak for grief.
They kneeled down at his feet
and begged him if it were his will
there to remain with them still.
"Leave off," he said, "it must be so."
All his kingdom he forsook
and only a pilgrim's cloak he took.
He had no tunic, and no hood,
no shirt and no other goods,
except his harp at any rate,
and barefoot went he out of the gate.
Oh woe what weeping and what grief was shown,
when he who'd worn the kingly crown,
went so poorly out of the town,
through the woods and over the heath,
into the wilderness took his grief.
Nothing he found could ease his way,
he lived in hardship and poverty.
He who had worn fine furs and pelts
and lain on a bed of soft purple silk,
now on the hard heath there he lies
and covers himself with grass and leaves.
He that had castles and towers tall,
rivers, forests, meadows and all,

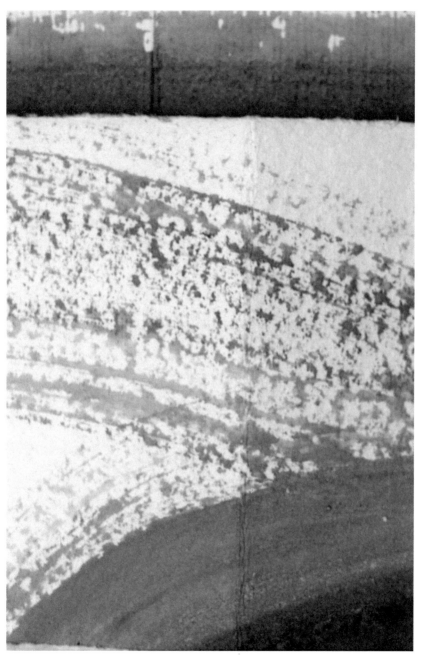

into the wilderness took his grief

now when it starts to snow and freeze
this king must make his bed of moss.
He that had all his noble knights
and ladies kneeling in his sight,
now sees nothing that pleases him
but only serpents slithering.
He that once had great plenty
of meat and drink so daintily,
all day now must dig and grub
before he can find his fill of roots.
In summertime he lives on wild fruits
and poor berries of little note.
In winter he finds nothing to eat
but grasses, and roots and bark for his meat.
His body has shrunken and dwindled away,
beaten by hardship, wind and rain.
Lord who can ever tell the pain
this king suffered for ten years more.
The hairs of his beard all rough and black
had grown down to his waist, alack.
His harp, in which was all his joy,
he hid in the hollow of a tree,
but when the weather was bright and clear
then at once he took up his harp so dear
and played for his own delight to hear.
The sound rang out through all the wood
and all the wild beasts came in a crowd
and gathered about him just to hear

now when it starts to snow and freeze

but when the weather was bright and clear

the King of Faery with his rout
riding to hunt all round about

and all the birds in all the air
came and sat on every thorn
to hear him play right through to the end
such a sweet melody there was born.
But when he ceased his harp to play
no beast would longer with him stay.
Sometimes he would see about his seat,
and often in the midday heat,
the King of Faery with his rout
riding to hunt all round about,
with faery cries and horns a-blowing
and with them hounds all loudly barking.
But never a beast did they seem to catch
nor after could he tell the way they took.
At other times he might seem to see
as if a great host passed him by,
a thousand knights all well turned out,
each armed to the teeth without a doubt.
Fierce and bold they were of face,
with banners flying in that place,
and everyone had his sword drawn
but he never knew where they had gone.
And sometimes he saw a stranger thing
knights and ladies all came dancing
richly attired in elegant dress,
with graceful and with courtly steps.
Pipes and drums passed him by
and every kind of minstrelsy.

Then one day he saw beside him
sixty ladies on horseback riding,
fair and happy as birds on the bough,
but never a man among them he saw,
and each had a falcon on her wrist.
Riding and hawking by the stream
there they found a plenty of game.
Mallards, herons and cormorants too,
the waterfowl away they flew
but the falcons tracked them down
and every falcon slew his own.
Orfeo laughed to see the sport.
"My faith," he said, "here's a good game.
There I'll go, in God's name!"
Then up he rose and there he went.
And soon alongside a lady he drew,
looked and saw and at once he knew
by every sign that indeed it was
his own dear queen Lady Herodis.
With joy he saw her and she him
but neither to other could speak a word.
The moss she could see upon her lord
who had been so rich and high
made the tears fall from her eye.
Seeing her weep, those ladies fair
forced her to ride away from there.
With him she could no longer stay.
"Alas," cried Orfeo, "for all my pain,

why has not death now me slain?
Alas wretch that you can't die
even after all this misery.
Alas, that still so long is my life
when to my very own dear wife,
I dare not one word speak, nor she to me.
Alas, why will my heart not break?
By God," he said, "whatever may be
and wherever may go these fair ladies
I will take that self same path,
and I care not whether to life or death."
He put on his pilgrim's cloak
and hung his harp upon his back,
and eagerly away he goes,
caring nothing for stumps and stones,
and when the ladies rode in at a rock
he followed after without any check.
And once inside the rock he saw,
when he had gone three miles or more,
he had come into a fair country
as bright as the sun on a summer's day
smooth and flat, and all so green
hill or dale was none to be seen.
And in the middle a castle he saw
rich and royal and wondrous tall.
All of the outer fortress wall
was clear and brilliant as any crystal.
A hundred towers there were about

with battlements so brave and stout.
The buttresses rising from the moat
were richly made of red gold bright.
Their arches too were all adorned
with coloured enamels of every kind.
Within the castle were spacious halls,
and precious stones enriched them all.
The least pillar you might behold
was also fashioned of burnished gold.
All that land was always light,
for, when it should be dark and night,
the precious stones so brightly shone
they made it as light as the noonday sun.
No one could tell or even conceive
the richness of the work, but believe
from everything there that it must be
the proud court of paradis.
The ladies alighted in this hall
and Orfeo followed after them all.
Orfeo knocked then at the gate
where the porter was ready to open it
and asked him what his business might be.
"By my faith, I am a minstrel," said he,
"to delight your master with my glee
if his sweet will that should be."
The porter undid the gate right fast
and let him into the castle pass.
When Orfeo began to look around

All that land was always light

he saw, lying upon the ground
within the wall, people falsely thither brought
when they were thought dead but they were not.
Some stood without a head,
and no arms others had.
Some had a body wound,
others were madmen bound.
Some sat armed on horse back,
others had choked as they ate.
Some were in water drowned,
others by a fire all burned.
Women in childbed lay,
some dead, some with their minds astray.
And a great many lay there beside
as if they slept at the noontide.
Each was taken out of the land
by the faery folk on every hand.
There he saw his very own wife,
Lady Herodis, his dearest life,
sleeping under the apple tree,
for by her clothes he knew it was she.
When he had seen all these marvellous things
he entered the hall that was the king's,
where he saw a splendid sight,
a canopy all fair and bright,
under which their lord, the king, was sat
and their queen so fair and sweet.
Their crowns and their clothes shone so bright

Orfeo could hardly bear the sight.
But when he had seen all those things
he kneeled down before the king.
"O Lord," he said, "if it would give you cheer,
my minstrelsy you now could hear!"
The king replied, "What man are you
that comes here now?
I, nor none that is with me here
ever sent for you to appear.
And never since I began to rule,
did I ever see such a fool
that dared to come here to me,
unless I sent for him specifically."
"Lord," said he, "please know well
I am only a poor minstrel.
And sire, know it's the custom with us
to seek out many a lord's house
though we might not be welcome there for long
yet we must offer them our song."
Before the king he then sat down
and took his harp with its tuneful sound
and tuned his harp, as well he can,
and lovely music he there began,
so that all in the palace drew near
and came to him so that they could hear,
and lay down at his very feet,
thinking his melody so sweet.
The king too listened and sat very still;

to hear the song was all his will.
Great pleasure he got there from the tune
and so too did his noble queen.
When Orfeo's harping ceased to sing
then these words spoke the Faery King.
"Minstrel I like your music so well
whatever you want of me now tell.
Generously I will pay you all
that you may ask. Now make your call."
"Sir," he said, "I beg of you
that you would give to me
that lady of the lovely hue
sleeping under the apple tree."
"Nay," said the king, "that cannot be.
A sorry couple you would make
for you are lean and rough and black.
She is lovely and flawless, as you may see.
A loathsome thing it would surely be
to see her in your company.'
"O sire," said Orfeo, "my gentle King,
but it would be a fouler thing
to hear a false word from your mouth.
So sire, since you said just now
whatever I asked I should have
you must keep the word you gave."
The king replied, "Since it is so
take her by the hand and go
and I wish you joy of her."

He kneeled down and thanked him there.
Then he took his dear wife by the hand
and hurried at once out of that land,
and out of that country too
as he had come, by the route he knew.
So in the end he found his way
and came to Winchester one day,
back to his very own city
but no one knew that it was he.
No further than the outskirts of town
he dare not go in case he was known
but in a beggar's house so mean
he took a lodging with his queen,
for himself and his dear wife,
as a minstrel of humble life,
and asked for news of that land
and who the kingdom had in hand.
The poor beggar in his shack
told him all, and how, alack,
their fair queen was stolen away
ten years ago by the King of Faery,
and how their own king had gone astray
but where to no one could ever say.
And how the steward the kingdom held
and many other things he told.
In the morning about noontide,
leaving his wife to stay behind,
the beggar's clothes he borrowed quick

and hung his harp around his neck,
and out he went to his own city
so that the people might him see.
Barons and earls of high degree,
merchants and ladies stared at him.
"Lord," they said, "what a strange man.
How long his hair hangs down so free,
and his beard has grown right to his knee,
while he himself is gnarled as a tree."
And as he went along the street,
with his own steward he chanced to meet
and cried out aloud to him:
"Sir steward, of your mercy hear me.
I am a harper from heathen lands.
Have pity, give me your helping hand."
The steward said, "Come with me, come.
Of all I have, you shall have some.
Every good harper has a welcome assured
for the love of Sir Orfeo, my own dear Lord."
In the castle the steward sat down to dine
with many a lording all so fine.
There were pipers and drummers,
many harpers and crowders,
and many were the tunes they played.
Orfeo listened but no word he said
but waited until all sounds should stop.
Then he took up and tuned his harp
and the sweetest notes he let fall there

and the sweetest notes he let fall there

that ever anyone might hear.
And all of them so liked his tune.
But the steward stared hard and very soon
he saw the harp and knew it full well.
"If you would thrive, minstrel, now tell
where you got this harp and how,
and I beg of you to tell me now."
"My Lord," he said, "in an unknown place,
as I went on my way through the wilderness,
there I found all in a dale
a man torn by lions into pieces small
and wolves had devoured him with their sharp teeth.
And this same harp beside him lay.
Over ten years ago it was, I say."
"O," said the steward, "to me what woe!
For this was my lord, Sir Orfeo.
Alas wretched man, what will you do
that are of such a lord forlorn?
Alas, the day that I was born,
and that such a hard fate was appointed him,
and he marked out for a death so grim."
Straightway he fell down in a trance.
His barons lifted him up at once,
and told him that's the way things are,
for a man's death there is no cure.
King Orfeo knew by this
his steward ever faithful was
and loved him as he ought to do.

He stood up then and said to them, "Lo,
see steward and listen to me now,
if I were your king, Sir Orfeo,
and had suffered for many years
in the wilderness of tears,
and had won my queen away,
from the land of the faery,
and had led her by the hand
right here to the city's end,
and, leaving her with a beggar man,
had myself come here again,
secretly in mean attire,
just to test your true desire,
and I found you to be so true,
you would never this day rue,
for certainly do not doubt this thing,
after my death you shall be king.
But if you'd been happy at my death
you'd very quickly soon have left."
When all those that were gathered then
understood it was Orfeo, their king,
and the steward knew without a doubt,
he ran to him, knocking the tables about,
to fall down at his feet,
and so did all who there were sat,
and all cried out the very same thing:
"You are our lord, Sir, and our king!"
They were so glad to see him alive

they led him to his own chamber
bathed and shaved him and cut his hair
and robed him as a king so fair.
And then in a great procession
they brought the queen into the town
with all sorts of minstrelsy.
With joy the tears fell from each one's eyes
that they were safely returned for all to see.
Now King Orfeo is newly crowned
with the Lady Herodis, his queen.
So they lived for many years again,
and afterward the steward did reign.
Harpers in Brittany after them
heard how this strange story began,
and made it into a song so pleasing
that it was named after the king;
and 'Orfeo' called because of him.
Fine is the song and sweet to sing.
And so came Orfeo out of all his cares.
God grant us all as well to fare.

Amen

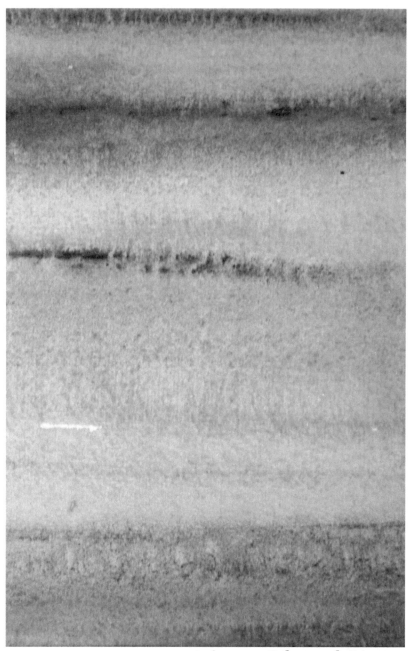

And so came Orfeo out of all his cares

Past Present: Piers Plowless & Sir Orfeo
by Maureen Duffy
is Pottery Press Pamphlet number

1

Other Pottery Press publications:

MOTHERTONGUE
Frances Bingham (poem) & Liz Mathews (images)

Paper Wings
Maureen Duffy (poems)
Liz Mathews (artist's book)

The Blue Hour of Natalie Barney
Frances Bingham (Pottery Press Pamphlet 2)

Under the Quarry Woods
Jeremy Hooker (prose poems) & Liz Mathews (images)
(Pottery Press Pamphlet 3)

THE
POTTERY
PRESS   www.pottersyard.co.uk